LONDON
IN
FIFTY
DESIGN
ICONS

**DESIGN
MUSEUM**

LONDON
IN
FIFTY
DESIGN
ICONS

**DEYAN
SUDJIC**

conran
OCTOPUS

LONDON

INTRODUCTION

By the standards of the world's endless megacities, London is manageable. Within its political boundaries, its population at around 8.5 million set against Tokyo's 40 million may seem modest, even if it is in reality a much larger settlement, spilling all the way from Reading in the west to Colchester in the east. But it is still larger than many nation states, and is regarded by its critics as if it were a huge and faceless urban sprawl, an anonymous city of strangers. In fact, London is anything but anonymous. It is a city with a powerful and distinctive identity that is uniquely its own, the product of its geography, history and climate that is reflected in everything from its skyline, to the quality of light over the river, and from its transport system to the typography used on its street signs.

Some of these markers are the product of self-conscious design decisions; others are the result of unintended consequences. For example, London is defined by the postal districts that were invented to make delivering mail easier, but which have produced clusters of letters that have metamorphosed into a kind of social register, separating the up-and-coming from the solidly wealthy, and the deprived from the bohemian. London is distilled in the heraldry of its football teams and in the design of the local newspaper that its citizens read. It is these elements at every scale, from the material used for its pavements, to the form taken by its clusters of skyscrapers, to the colour of its buses that give shape and identity to a city. They are elements that serve to create a sense of belonging, of showing what London is, and what it is not.

The term 'icon' in the architectural sense was hijacked in the wake of the completion of Frank Gehry's Guggenheim Museum in Bilbao. Iconic became synonymous with exhibitionism. The 50 icons in this book are to be understood in a different sense. Each in its own way is a distinctive expression of a different aspect of the city's character. Some of them appear throughout London, serving to define the grain of the city. Others are the landmarks that define London internationally. Some have been deliberately created; others are the unselfconscious products of pragmatic decisions that have come to be seen as uniquely part of London. There are both masterpieces and banalities. All serve to define and explain the city's exceptional character.

Sir Christopher Wren's dome for St Paul's is the defining element in the city's historic skyline. Norman Foster and the engineers from Arup designed the pedestrian bridge that links the cathedral and the City of London, with Southwark and Tate Modern.

CHRISTOPHER WREN
Creator of a landmark for the city

London without Christopher Wren is unthinkable. A 17th-century scientist who trained himself how to design buildings in Oxford and Cambridge, Wren came to London in the wake of the Great Fire and gave the city its structure and its monuments.

The building of St Paul's, on the ruins of the medieval gothic cathedral that once stood on the site, started in 1675 and is one of the greatest achievements of Western civilization. The cathedral served as the prototype for, and the summation of, the scores of city churches that Wren designed with much less pain and suffering, and today its dome still serves to define the city and its architecture.

Wren provided a model for generations of architect-city builders that followed him. He gave Nicholas Hawksmoor his chance. And Hawksmoor built some of London's most wonderful baroque buildings in its expanding East End, the best of which is Christ Church in Spitalfields – a complex mix of aesthetic impulses that so inspired the architect James Stirling that he chose it as his last resting place.

During World War II, at the time of the Blitz, a generation of elderly architectural historians were ready to risk their lives to save St Paul's as they kept watch for incendiary bombs.

Christopher Wren's dome for St Paul's marked London's reconstruction after the Great Fire of 1666, and its survival of the 1940–1 Blitz.

THE PUB
The end of the public house

For generations the London pub has been lamented as doomed and dying. And yet it still survives. As long ago as the 1950s, the editors of the *Architectural Review* created their idealized version of a pub in the basement of their offices on Queen Anne's Gate, decorating it with fragments salvaged from the Blitz, stuffed lions and all the cut-glass mirrors you could shake a stick at. Their magazine expressed its dismay as brewery chains standardized once distinctively individual pubs and lamented the impossibility of creating a modern equivalent that could rival the splendour of its Victorian forebears.

Of all the pubs that remain, the Prospect of Whitby is perhaps the one to single out, though not because it has been redeemed by the quality of its food or by the strength of the local community – Wapping is not what it once was. However, the Prospect is *old*, a place that has been intimately linked with the Thames trade, and the grey river sky, since the 16th century. And it also earned its place in history when it was blown up in the film *The Long Good Friday* (1980) – not the Prospect itself, of course, but a renamed lookalike built at the other end of Wapping Wall.

Under threat from changing social customs, and the appeal of wine over beer, the pub is in decline, yet at times retains its charm.

TRAFALGAR SQUARE
The hero on the column

Trafalgar Square was laid out in the first half of the 19th century, on land left vacant by the transfer of the royal mews to Pimlico. John Nash was the first architect involved. He worked on the road layouts that connected the area with his master plan, which stretched all the way north to Camden by way of Haymarket, Piccadilly Circus, Regent Street, Portland Place and The Regent's Park. Trafalgar Square was envisaged as a point on the route south towards Westminster and The Mall. It was a vision that inspired the exiled French Emperor Napoleon III to go home and remodel Paris in an even more monumental manner.

The dominant piece of architecture in the square is the National Gallery, designed by William Wilkins, with Robert Venturi and Denise Scott Brown's Sainsbury Wing making a later appearance as a coda to postmodernism. The square itself is the work of Charles Barry. South Africa House, designed by Herbert Baker, is on the east side, faced by Canada House, designed by Robert Smirke. Norman Foster carried out a partial pedestrianization that saw traffic excluded from the northern edge.

As a site of political protest, Trafalgar Square seems to have lost the vitality that it had in the 19th and 20th centuries. This was where William Morris addressed a huge crowd in the aftermath of the Bloody Sunday riot of 1887; where protestors demanded 'Law not War' during the Suez Crisis in 1956; and where the Campaign for Nuclear Disarmament rallied hundreds of thousands throughout the 1960s.

Here, public sculpture is alive and well. The 'fourth plinth', in the northwest corner, was intended for an equestrian statue of William IV, the brother of Nash's great patron, George IV. But after the monarch died, and his architect became embroiled in a scandal over cost overruns on Buckingham Palace, the money to make it was never raised. In the last 20 years the plinth has been used for specially commissioned temporary art installations.

Every year that a new succession of artists is unveiled, the same arguments break out. Progressives propose clearing out the forgotten admirals and minor members of the royal family commemorated in bronze that clutter the square. Conservatives lament the facetiousness of the work on the fourth plinth.

Britain's most famous admiral, Horatio Nelson, is memorialized in the most un-British way, impaled on top of a surrealistic out-of-scale Corinthian column, in the middle of Trafalgar Square. Far below him, the 'fourth plinth' is a model of what contemporary public art can achieve. Katharina Fritsch's *Hahn/Cock*, 2013 (below), is but one example.

GIN BOTTLE
London's ruin

Exactly how London developed its appetite for gin is a
contested history, but the Netherlands features in most accounts.
The Dutch were drinking clear distilled spirits flavoured with
botanicals long before the British. In some versions, it was English
troops supporting their Protestant allies who acquired a taste for
jenever while helping to defend Amsterdam from the Spanish.
The assumption of the British throne by William of Orange is also
said to have played an important part in the popularity of gin in
London. Gin turned from a medicinal tonic to a cheap route to
stupefaction, its popularity deplored by William Hogarth in his
acid depiction of the miseries it caused in his 1751 print *Gin Lane*.

Over the years, gin became the basis for the gin martini in
the United States, a drink that made it east across the Atlantic.
As the only prophylactic for malaria in the colonial era, the
quinine that was added to tonic water tasted uncomfortably
bitter. Adding gin provided a welcome distraction, and it went
on to prove a popular drink.

For 20 years gin became a pariah among spirits, shouldered
aside by flavourless vodka, or even by tequila. Eventually,
Beefeater became the only 'London gin' (a designation based
on flavour) that was still being distilled on an industrial scale
in the capital. And then, to demonstrate that there are fashions
for alcohol just as there are for everything else, came the new
explosion of artisan-made gin in London.

Hogarth's vision of *Gin
Lane* was not satire, but
an impassioned attack on
the gin-drinking epidemic
of his times, and the social
damage that it caused.
A more sober London has
recently re-established gin
as a mark of its identity.

GIN LANE.

SIR JOHN SOANE'S MUSEUM
The home of the architect

Sir John Soane designed a string of stately homes, the Bank of England, and remodelled the Houses of Parliament before they caught fire in 1832 and were comprehensively rebuilt. The tomb that he designed for himself – which still stands in the graveyard of the church of St Pancras – provided the model for the telephone box designed by Giles Gilbert Scott. But it is his own home that is his most lasting memorial.

Disappointed by his children, one of whom actually went so far as to publish anonymous criticism of his father's work in London's newspapers, Soane disinherited them and spent his not inconsiderable fortune on an extraordinary collection of art and artefacts, from ancient sarcophagi to William Hogarth's *A Rake's Progress*, and on acquiring three houses on the north side of Lincoln's Inn Fields that he needed to accommodate it.

Soane's collection, spiced with models of his own work and the painted representations of them executed by his loyal assistant and draughtsman, Joseph Michael Gandy, is remarkable. But even more astonishing is Soane's remodelling of the interiors of his home, creating a series of sensational and ambiguous spaces that seem far removed from the ostensibly neoclassical restraint of his architectural language.

Sir John Soane, architect of the Bank of England, turned his own home on Lincoln's Inn Fields into a museum dedicated to his work, and his eclectic collection of art and artefacts.

THE REGENT'S PARK
Planning the great city

The Regent's Park began as a huge residential property speculation in the early years of the 19th century. It has since become a key part of London's most essential feature: its network of parks, which today makes it one of Europe's greenest capitals.

Conceived by John Nash for his patron, the Prince Regent, The Regent's Park is a defining piece of picturesque city planning. It was intended to give London the impetus to leap across the Marylebone Road and expand towards its northern suburbs.

The park was to be edged by a series of grand stucco-faced terraces that gave individual houses the aspect of a palace. Nash designed a number of the terraces himself, deploying giant classical orders, pediments and rooftop sculpture. However, much of the housing was in fact built by developers who had bought up the surrounding plots of land. Some of these deliberately flouted Nash's stylistic guidelines, which accounts for the sudden shift from sandstone French Empire style, to white stucco classicism, to grey-brick gothic along the eastern edge.

London Zoo occupies the northern edge of the park. And in recent years the park has become home to the annual Frieze Art Fair with its sequence of architect-designed tents.

At the start of the 19th century, John Nash turned the suburban fringe north of central London into a landscaped park, ringed by palatial terraced houses, that became a worldwide model for city planning.

TOWER BRIDGE
A bridge like no other

There is nothing else in the world quite like Tower Bridge (built 1886–94). It is the product of the very particular circumstances of London at the end of the 19th century when the Thames was full of shipping from all over the world and the city's population had doubled in four decades. A new crossing to link the north and south banks, just to the east of the Tower of London – to ease congestion on existing bridges – had been in discussion ever since 1870. The difficulty was how to thread it through one of the busiest ports in the world without disturbing the shipping. A bridge high enough to allow tall ships under it was suggested by Sir Joseph Bazalgette, but that would have needed a 1,524m- (5,000ft-) long spiralling ramp.

The most practical solution was a bridge that could be opened and closed with hydraulic power. But because the Thames Conservancy insisted that the bridge be opened for two hours each day, there was also a need for a high-level pedestrian walkway. That, and the fact that the Crown insisted that the bridge reflected the architecture of the Tower of London, accounts for the remarkable silhouette of the bridge.

Inside the crenellations and turrets of the granite skin is a steel structure – entertainingly revealed in one of the more imaginative sequences of Guy Ritchie's *Sherlock Holmes* (2009). The hydraulics are capable of opening the bridge in less than five minutes, which made the high-level walkway redundant. The wharves upstream of the bridge have gone, too. What is left is a remarkable monument to what London once was and an internationally recognizable logo for the city as it is today.

Under its gothic granite skin, Tower Bridge is a triumph of Victorian engineering. It was designed on two levels: a deck for vehicles that could open to allow ships to pass through and a high-level pedestrian walkway, which subsequently fell into disuse.

BOROUGH MARKET
A revival south of the river

Food markets are the essential engines of any city. In London, they were once close to transport routes. A thousand years ago it was the Thames. Then came canals and railways. Now the markets, or the distribution centres that have succeeded them, have migrated to the giant sheds that have appeared at the edges of the motorway network.

They have left behind what are mainly 19th-century buildings, now recycled for new, often ornamental, uses. Billingsgate near the Tower of London once sold fish. Now it is an events space. There are no fruit and vegetable stands in Covent Garden market, just a huge Apple Store and a Burberry outlet. At Smithfield's, the meat trade is under threat.

Borough Market, caught in a tangle of railway viaducts and medieval streets, is more interesting. There have been markets hereabouts for many centuries. The buildings that remain are mostly from the 1850s and 1860s, to which a swaggering art deco entrance was added after World War I. The old traders have been surrounded by the cult of food. The balance is tipping towards spectators rather than participants, but this is still a place to eat well and to experience the grain of an older city.

Once a commercial fruit and vegetable market that supplied London's greengrocers, Borough Market has turned food into a spectator sport.

GREENWICH MERIDIAN
A walk along the world's timeline

The idea that time and space are calibrated in terms of their relationship in degrees east and west of Greenwich, the south-east suburb of London from which the Royal Navy set out to rule the waves in the 18th century, seems so fixed and permanent. It is easy to forget that it was only in 1884 that the Prime Meridian was defined by the location of the large 'Transit Circle' telescope in the Royal Observatory, originally planned by Christopher Wren and Robert Hooke in 1675. The Transit Circle itself was built by Sir George Biddell Airy, the seventh Astronomer Royal, in 1850 and was to have huge consequences.

Defining a single meridian took several decades of technical, but also strategic, negotiation. The political sensitivities of those nations that believed they had a claim to be seen as being at the centre of the world needed to be smoothed over. In particular, France, which maintained its own Paris meridian until 1914, had to be pacified. But, without a single point of reference, the scope for chaos was huge. In the United States the railway companies had to deal with four different time zones, and there was an urgent demand for consistency. An international conference was convened in 1884 to build a consensus in favour of one point of measurement. London's global position, and its history of recordkeeping, made it the pre-eminent choice.

Outside the observatory at Greenwich, a brass strip marks out the invisible line dividing eastern and western hemispheres, seeming to connect the Royal Observatory with the towers of Canary Wharf – down the hill and across the Thames – and then on into the infinite distance.

An invisible line made visible: used since the 18th century by sailors to find their way around the world, the Prime Meridian is commemorated in a brass strip in the Royal Observatory courtyard.

Colombo 79° 51' E
Bombay 72° 51' E
Addis Abeba 38° 43' E
Saigon 106° 43' E
Bangkok 100° 30' E
Rangoon 96° 10' E
Hanoi 105° 51' E
Hong Kong 114° 11' E
Riyadh 46° 46' E
Cairo 31° 15' E
Jerusalem 35° 13' E
Tehran 51° 26' E
Tokyo 139° 45' E
Seoul 127° 00' E
Athens 23° 44' E
Beijing 116° 25' E
Istanbul 28° 57' E
Rome 12° 30' E
Berlin 13° 25' E
Amsterdam 4° 52' E
Greenwich 00° 00'
Paris 2° 20' E

Accra 00° 00' W
Panama 79° 32' W
Caracas 66° 50' W
Barbados 59° 30' W
Kingston 76° 48' W
Mexico City 99° 10' W
Honolulu 157° 50' W
Havana 82° 25' W
Bahamas 78° 00' W
Bermuda 64° 30' W
Dallas 96° 48' W
Casablanca 7° 35' W
Los Angeles 118° 15' W
Lisbon 9° 08' W
Washington 77° 00' W
Madrid 3° 43' W
New York 73° 50' W
Chicago 87° 45' W
Ottawa 75° 43' W
Montreal 73° 34' W
Greenwich 00° 00' W

SELFRIDGES & CO.
The retail palace

Mixing luxury retailing with social diversions, the department store has its roots in Printemps and Bon Marché of Paris and was perfected in the United States. London created three examples with enough allure to become international trophies: Harvey Nichols is now Chinese owned; Harrods was acquired by Qatari investors from the Egyptian Al Fayed; and Selfridges is owned by the Canadian Weston family.

In the early 20th century Harry Gordon Selfridge revolutionized British retailing with his American panache and taste for grandiloquent architecture.

Selfridges is the most interesting of the three, in part because of its roots. Gordon Selfridge came to London from the United States in 1908, bringing the noted Chicago architect Daniel Burnham with him to build a palatial store on Oxford Street. This was graced by Gilbert Bayes' 3.6m- (11ft-) high polychrome sculpture *The Queen of Time* and a stately parade of giant ionic columns.

Despite its handsome architecture, Selfridges, like many department stores, went through a rough patch in the 1970s. It has since been brought back from retailing irrelevance, however. Its original spaces have re-emerged from unsympathetic alterations, and the owners have managed to recapture some of the sense of spectacle that made the original department stores such successful attractions.

SELFRIDGE & Co., Ltd., OXFORD STREET, LONDON, W.

(Midway between Bond Street and Marble Arch).

The Largest Stocks and Assortments in London of Drapery, Outfitting, Clothing, etc., including nearly everything required for daily use of Ladies, Gentlemen, and Children (except Groceries, etc.), at *London's Lowest Prices always.*

TUBE MAP
Defining London

London is defined and given shape and identity by the map of its underground railway system. The Metropolitan line began operating in 1863, with open coaches drawn by coal-burning, steam-powered locomotives running between Paddington and Aldgate East. It took Paris 50 years to catch up.

What had started out as a cluster of privately owned underground lines turned, in the early 20th century, into a municipal, coherently run system under the direction of Frank Pick. Described by the architectural historian Nikolaus Pevsner as 'a modern Medici', Pick commissioned austere new stations from Charles Holden, an elegant font designed by Edwin Johnston, a distinctive circle and bar logotype, and posters by everybody from Edward McKnight Kauffer to László Moholy-Nagy. But perhaps the most powerful achievement was the London Underground map – a diagram, really – produced not by a designer at all but by Harry Beck, an engineering draughtsman working in London Transport's signals office.

From 1933 onward the new Underground map created the mental image of what London is – a symbol, but also a means of understanding how to navigate the city. There is something of Beck's background in drawing electrical circuit diagrams in the way that the interchanges are described by open circles, but the real insight was the way in which the river Thames appears on the map – a reminder of actual geography that roots the diagram in reality.

It was the point of departure for every other subway system map in the world. Massimo Vignelli's work for New York's subway system had much more gorgeous citrus colours, but lasted less than five years. Beck's work has inspired artists and attracted the attention of Marxist-leaning design historians, who have suggested that the diagram was used by unscrupulous house builders to suggest that the new housing estates they were throwing up around the stations at the end of the lines were much closer to the city centre than they actually were.

Harry Beck's artless draughtsmanship served to define the geography of modern London, not with a map, but through the clarity of a diagram. Under the leadership of Frank Pick, every aspect of the London Underground was carefully designed to create a single coherent identity, from the architecture of Tube stations to the signage (below).

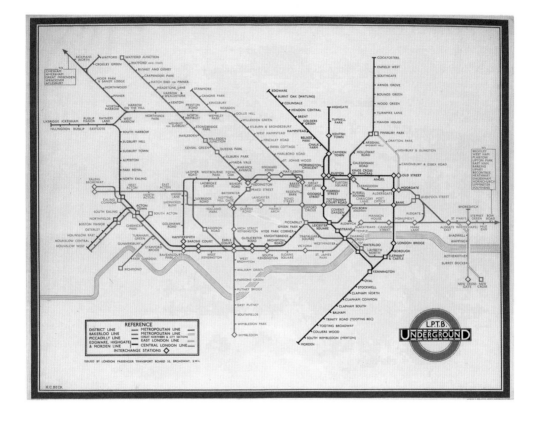

CHELSEA SHIRT
From the pensioner to the lion

Football in London was once a working-class pursuit, played by part-timers with day jobs, in shorts that came down to their knees. They Brylcreemed their hair and smoked Capstan Full Strength cigarettes. And they were called Nobby. Matches were watched from the terraces by men who wore cloth caps. There were no seats – everybody stood. It was only the middle classes who had the leisure time to watch cricket matches that could last three days from the comfort of fixed seats.

By the late 1960s the traditional audience for football was being superseded by the skinhead cult. Its adepts wore checked Ben Sherman button-down shirts and braces that held up faded Levi's that stopped an inch above their cherry-red boots. In those days, when Geoff Hurst and the team played in mid-table Second Division, Chelsea was followed by a particularly aggressive variant, who left their tags sprayed over west London walls and gathered in the home stand, The Shed, kept apart from the away fans by mounted police.

But, despite the violence, Chelsea was one of the most visible football clubs in the world. By the time that Tony Blair's New Labour came to power, the aggression had been brought under control and ex-public-school boys were claiming to be devoted football followers, too. As in Blair's own case, they were sometimes a little shaky about the exact details. Roman Abramovich, one of a number of Russian oligarchs to relocate to London, bought Chelsea in 2003.

Under Abramovich, Chelsea players were as likely to have been born in Côte d'Ivoire as in west London, but he did bring back the lion that the club used on its shirt in the 1950s – when it had replaced the original emblem featuring a less-than-macho Chelsea Pensioner. Chelsea, however, has always played in blue shirts.

Long before a Russian oligarch acquired Chelsea Football Club, Jimmy Greaves in his blue shirt and long white shorts defined the essence of traditional football, even though he wore the club's lion insignia, rather than the original version of a Chelsea Pensioner.

GREEN BELT
Taming the endless city

The Metropolitan Green Belt stretches over almost 5,180km^2 (2,000 square miles), distributed on the outer edges of 19 London boroughs and neighbouring bits of the counties of Bedfordshire, Berkshire, Buckinghamshire, Essex, Hertfordshire, Kent and Surrey. In this form, the idea of a Green Belt goes back to 1938, when it was introduced as a measure to prevent so-called ribbon development spreading along the numerous arterial roads radiating out of London.

Authorities of one kind or another have been trying to stop London from growing all the way back to Tudor times. Then it was an attempt to stop citizenry escaping the clutches of tax-raising powers; now it is presented as a means of protecting the countryside. Under its shelter come the water meadows around Runnymede, the elegant grounds of Hampton Court, and the North Downs.

London as a reality, if not necessarily as a political entity, has clearly leapfrogged the restraints of the Green Belt. 'London' is a 160-km (100-mile) sprawl that stretches all the way from Bournemouth to Ipswich, defined by commuting distances and house prices. When the High Speed 2 railway is built, London and Birmingham will come closer than ever to being merged. With the painful inability of London to create affordable housing, the role of the belt in distorting the market for housing will be called more and more into question.

Ever since the Middle Ages, London's apparently unstoppable growth has troubled governments worried that they would lose tax revenue. The Metropolitan Green Belt, created after World War II, was designed to ease the concerns of London's commuters that the suburbs would lose their rural character.

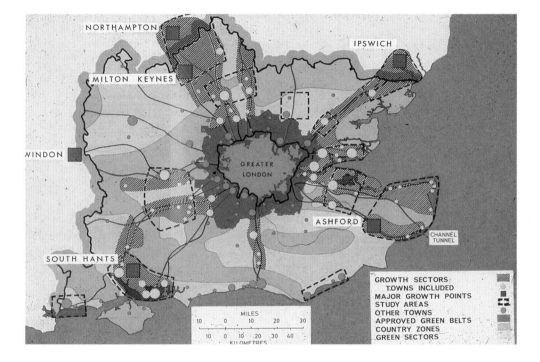

NORTHAMPTON

MILTON KEYNES

IPSWICH

WINDON

GREATER
LONDON

ASHFORD

CHANNEL
TUNNEL

SOUTH HANTS

MILES
10   0   10   20   30

10   0   10   20   30   40
KILOMETRES

GROWTH SECTORS
T.OWNS INCLUDED
MAJOR GROWTH POINTS
STUDY AREAS
OTHER TOWNS
APPROVED GREEN BELTS
COUNTRY ZONES
GREEN SECTORS

LONDON TAXI
A comfortable retreat on wheels

The London taxi is so quietly distinctive that it has become a defining part of the city's urban landscape – so much so that there is a case to be made for English Heritage to give it the same protection it offers listed buildings. And yet, in its most traditional form, it is in trouble.

There was a period during the 1970s when third-hand versions, so badly maintained that the London Carriage Office could have had them taken off the streets on sight, were seen cruising the streets of Belfast as the Provisional IRA's preferred means of transport. That indignity has passed and the current version of the taxi, tailor-made to the capital's specifications, is one of a sequence of cabs that goes back to at least the 1930s.

The cleverest thing about the current model, the TX4 (essentially a development of Kenneth Grange's TX1 of 1997), is the way that the designer has managed to make it look as though it has been around forever without making it feel like a living fossil – unlike its closest relative, New York's now-defunct Checker Cab. With its ability to seat five in comfort, the TX4 is the closest thing to a Pall Mall gentleman's club on wheels.

Manganese Bronze, the company that makes the TX4 in Coventry, has had technical problems with the power steering that gives the taxi its famous 7.5m (25ft) turning circle. Technically, it does not match up to less distinguished rivals – off-the-peg imports from Germany and Japan. GPS is making the 'Knowledge' – so patiently acquired by taxi drivers before they can qualify for a licence – superfluous; and disruptive Internet booking services are making them financially uncompetitive.

London's charismatic black taxi is the product of a strict set of rules defining its turning circle and interior arrangements. Over the generations it has gone through various incarnations, yet remained essentially the same. But its future is now under threat.

PEVSNER'S *LONDON*

According to Pevsner

Nikolaus Pevsner was a German art historian who came to Britain as a refugee in 1933. Having previously concentrated on baroque painting, his focus now shifted to contemporary architecture. As an editor at the *Architectural Review* and as an academic, he became closely associated with the attempt to convince Britain of the importance of a particularly austere version of modernism. But Pevsner was also a founder member of the Victorian Society, established in 1957 in a bid to stop the demolition of some of London's most outstanding landmarks.

His abiding legacy, however, is the monumental book series, 'The Buildings of England', a project with which he was involved from its beginnings in 1945 until his death in 1983, having written 32 of them himself and collaborated on 10 others. He dealt with London in two volumes. The first, called *London* – covering everything except the 'cities' of London and Westminster – was initially published in 1952. With its indefatigable research and wealth of detail, this served to define the architecture of the capital. Its pocket-size format was equally distinctive.

The London volumes have now swelled to six, a measure both of the sheer size of the capital and the ongoing revision of the material. Pevsner has often been mischaracterized as a dry academic, but his judgements on London are often vivid (e.g. 'the South Bank is brutalism at its most brutal'). He also opened the way for one of the most eloquent among his former collaborators, Ian Nairn, to publish a very different guide, *Nairn's London* (1968).

The sharp judgements of Nikolaus Pevsner's *London* volumes, originally part of Penguin's 'The Buildings of England' series, opened the city's eyes to its architectural glories and failures.

THE
BUILDINGS
OF
ENGLAND

London
except the Cities of London and Westminster

PENGUIN BOOKS

6/-

ROUTEMASTER
The view from the top deck

Who would have believed a commitment to resurrecting London's double-decker buses could underpin a mayoral election campaign? Boris Johnson's years in office are marked by fiascos such as the almost unused cable car crossing from the Greenwich Peninsula. The so-called 'Boris bikes' were mooted by his predecessor, Ken Livingstone, and based on what Paris had already done. But there is one London symbol for which Johnson is undoubtedly responsible: the Thomas Heatherwick-designed new Routemaster.

On Livingstone's watch, Transport for London replaced its Routemaster fleet – designed and built specifically for the city – with a German import, a single-deck coach dismissively referred to as the 'bendy bus' that was so long it often blocked crossroads. Johnson committed himself to a modernized Routemaster, which he pitched as an essential part of the city's identity.

The original Routemaster bus was prototyped in 1954. Mechanically, it was the work of a team led by London Transport's chief engineer, Albert Arthur Molteno Durrant (who designed tanks during World War II), Eric Ottoway and Colin Curtis. They used an aluminium body, power steering and an automatic gearbox that made it much lighter and easier to drive than its predecessors, even though it accommodated 64 passengers, 8 more than the model that it replaced.

But it was the industrial designer Douglas Scott, brought in as a consultant to style it, who made it such a charismatic distillation of London, one that still looks contemporary when it makes an occasional appearance on the city's heritage routes. Scott had worked for Raymond Loewy and restyled the Aga. He was determined that his bus would not look like a shoebox, as he put it, and gave it subtle tapered lines and curved edges. The interior was to project comfort and quality. The two decks were called 'saloons' and had what Scott called 'burgundy' lining panels, 'Chinese green' window surrounds and 'Sung yellow' ceilings. The seats had a specially designed tartan moquette with leather edges and there was a bell on a rope and a special box for used tickets.

The Routemaster bus became an archetype that helped brand London. Boris Johnson tried to replicate it during his time as mayor with Thomas Heatherwick's version (below).

HEATHROW
When the airport was young

Even with Beijing, Dubai and Atlanta snapping at its heels, Heathrow Airport remains the world's busiest in terms of international passenger traffic. It was the first model for the airport of the jet age, even if it was born out of a World War II-era runway built for heavy bombers. In its first incarnation, characterized by Frederick Gibberd's original terminal, opened in 1955, it was a vision of the modern world when air travel was for a privileged few. That terminal, subsequently demolished in 2010, was re-designated Terminal 2. Heathrow now has no fewer than five terminals, generates tens of thousands of jobs, and processes 70 million passengers every year.

In the formless, shapeless London of the 21st century, Heathrow has become a kind of surrogate for the lost public realm of the city. It is a landmark that acts as a kind of gateway to the city, a front door for Britain, continually slipping into squalor when it is overwhelmed by sheer numbers, only to be rescued by periodic bursts of reconstruction.

Heathrow, based on a World War II airbase, swiftly became one of the world's busiest international airports. Traces of the original building, designed by Frederick Gibberd, have all but disappeared under continual waves of rebuilding and expansion.

EMBASSY OF THE UNITED STATES
Under the eagle

Eero Saarinen was an American-Finnish architect who died painfully young in 1961, at the age of 51. He had not had the time to define his architectural identity, moving instead from the shell roofs of the TWA terminal at Kennedy Airport in New York to the Miesian austerity of his work for General Motors.

The Embassy of the United States in Grosvenor Square is his only work in Britain. It is a relic of a very particular moment in history. The site was donated to the United States as part of Britain's repayments of its lend-lease debts after World War II. It was an attempt to replicate the proportions of Georgian London's facades. But with its outstretched golden-eagle wings, surmounting an entrance no longer considered secure enough to use, it was also a monumental assertion of American power, and its relationship with its most troublesome, but devoted, European ally.

And now that the United States has decided that it needs a more defensible location for its embassy, even in the relative calm of London, the fate of the old building is a reflection of the new realities of the city. The embassy is moving south of the river, and Saarinen's landmark is now, like so many trophy buildings in London, and indeed in Europe, the property of Qatar's state-controlled investment fund.

The US Embassy in Grosvenor Square is Eero Saarinen's only building in the UK.

BT TOWER
The privatized monument

What was once called the Post Office Tower is now known as the BT Tower – a reflection of the privatization of Britain's public utilities in the Thatcher era when the Post Office's telecommunications arm was sold off. Its opening in 1964 by Harold Wilson, the prime minister of the time, created a new landmark for London that rose to a height of 191m (627ft). Its completion was a reflection of a brief moment of blithe optimism about progress, before the future finally lost its charm. It was the embodiment of what Wilson described as the 'white heat of the technological revolution'.

Culturally, the Post Office Tower was a dramatic turning point in another way. For the first time in four centuries, Sir Christopher Wren's dome of St Paul's was no longer the tallest structure in London. The tower was tall enough to provide line-of-sight transmission of microwave signals from the array of dishes that were attached to the slender concrete structure and could be directed north over the top of the Chiltern Hills.

The architect, Eric Bedford of the Ministry of Public Building and Works, treated the project as though it was a conventional office tower, with a glass curtain wall wrapped around the structure. It was crowned by a revolving restaurant operated (with particular bathos) by Butlins, the holiday camp group. For security reasons first the restaurant and then the tower were closed to the public at the beginning of the 1980s. However, despite the enormously rapid pace of technological change that has seen the microwave dishes stripped away, the tower is still used for communications transmission.

For three decades, London's tallest structure was what was once called the Post Office Tower. Its strategic significance meant that it was not shown on maps.

ROUNDHOUSE
Reclaiming the past

Originally opened in 1847 as an engine shed, servicing locomotives pulling trains out of Euston Station, the Roundhouse is exactly what its name suggests – a circular brick structure, under a slate roof, which once had an iron turntable at its centre allowing for locomotives to manoeuvre in and out. It became a warehouse less than a decade after it was opened, as engines grew more powerful and too large to be accommodated inside. For 50 years it was a storehouse for a London gin distillery.

The Roundhouse found a new life when the left-wing playwright Arnold Wesker established it as Centre 42, an arts centre, in 1964, named after a resolution passed by the Trades Union Congress calling for the arts to be made accessible beyond the traditional elite.

The Roundhouse's transformation was a very early example of the idea of recycling redundant structures without obvious architectural qualities for creative new uses. It metamorphosed into a focus of the counterculture: Jimi Hendrix, Pink Floyd, the Incredible String Band and even Marc Bolan, when T. Rex was still playing acoustic instruments, all appeared here.

The Roundhouse is now a performance venue, with a commitment to engaging with disadvantaged young people, in the midst of what has turned into one of London's most visited tourist hot spots – Camden Lock – selling T-shirts, piercings, street food and every conceivable variety of tattoo.

Camden's Roundhouse began life as an engine shed, then became a warehouse, and has now been converted into a performance space.

BARBICAN
Romantic modernism

Conceived out of the rubble of World War II, the Barbican was central London's biggest single attempt at the grand gesture of modernist planning. The City of London, the shadowy but powerful entity with an electorate so small that the usual tribulations of democratic politics do not apply, set about the reconstruction of an area on the northern edge of the Square Mile that had once been the parade ground of Roman legionaries. The idea was to combine a new residential community, crowned by three high-rise apartment towers, with a whole range of cultural amenities, as well as public open spaces and the City's school for girls.

Designed by the architectural practice Chamberlin, Powell and Bon, one of the foremost proponents of modernism in post-war Britain, the Barbican is a remarkable exercise in high-density urbanism. The architects used exposed concrete throughout, usually a bleak material, but by giving the towers a bold geometry based on a triangular plan as well as projecting balconies they managed to create a picturesque silhouette for the development when seen against the skyline.

The Barbican has withstood the whims of architectural fashion, the hard-to-navigate confusion of its art gallery, concert hall and theatre, and even a bad case of leaking flat roofs, to win over a sceptical London public.

The distinctive serrated silhouettes of the Barbican's high-rise towers make a remarkable landmark and, for once in the City of London, represent affordable housing rather than commerce.

ROYAL COLLEGE OF ART
An elite school for visual culture

A legacy of Henry Cole's vision, the Royal College of Art (RCA) was established in the wake of the Great Exhibition. It was intended for the education of the artists and designers that Britain would need if its products were to compete on a global scale. Its current incarnation as the world's only all-postgraduate art school, together with its building on Kensington Gore, is largely the work of one of its rectors, Charles Darwin, who in the years following World War II set out to create an elite school with the trappings of an ancient university, complete with college silver and senior common room.

The RCA has had a quite remarkable record in producing graduates who have gone on to dominate the world of visual culture. Graduates include David Hockney, James Dyson, Jasper Morrison, Tracey Emin, Konstantin Grcic, Robin Day and Daniel Weil. Ron Arad, when he was running the RCA's design product school, used to suggest that his job was to make his students unemployable. That is to say: he encouraged them to question all assumptions so that, in the process, they would be the kind of people who employed others.

Christopher Frayling, another former rector, once claimed that, while the Bauhaus produced lots of famous professors, the RCA is a place that has continuously produced students who became famous. The building itself was designed by H T Cadbury-Brown.

London's art schools, which attract talented students from around the world, have played a vital part in creating its international reputation as a creative centre. The RCA produced, among many others, John Pasche, whose 1971 lips and tongue design (right) has become synonymous with the Rolling Stones.

TIME OUT
On the masthead

Time Out magazine is a reminder of London's radical 1960s. In a fit of hippy utopianism, Tony Elliott started it as a collective in 1968 with the aim of publishing listings of all things groovy every fortnight. It covered T. Rex in their acoustic phase, playing at the Roundhouse, and Pink Floyd at the Middle Earth, a psychedelic club that opened in Covent Garden before the vegetable market had moved out.

It was quick to list gay and lesbian venues and to cover radical politics, and it rarely sold more than 5,000 copies. By the 1970s it was becoming more business-like, but to do so it had to survive a bruising strike by its original staff, their launch of a left-wing alternative (*City Limits*) when they decided to abandon the strike, and an opportunistic and short-lived commercial competitor launched by Richard Branson.

It was during this period that the graphic designer Pearce Marchbank gave *Time Out* its distinctive identity, in particular its masthead, that now appears on editions, some licensed, others subsidiaries, that appear around the world. *Time Out* gave a certain kind of London a sense of itself, making a shared view of the city visible. The magazine both reflected and helped to shape the London of its day.

The original London edition continues to flourish, in a new incarnation since 2012 as a free listings magazine, shorn of politics and handed out at every Tube station.

Tony Elliot created *Time Out* magazine. Pearce Marchbank designed the masthead that is now used around the world, and created some of its most distinctive covers.

Time Out
LONELY HEARTS
What Really Happens When You Answer An Ad

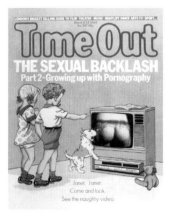

Time Out
THE SEXUAL BACKLASH
Part 2 - Growing up with Pornography

Janet, Janet
Come and look.
See the naughty video.

Time Out
Dial - A - Service
Where to get anything hired, done, fixed and fitted.

Time Out
McCARTNEY
DO YOU STILL NEED ME,
NOW IT'S '84?

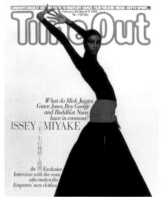

Time Out
What do Mick Jagger,
Grace Jones, Boy George
and Buddhist Nuns
have in common?
ISSEY MIYAKE

An Exclusive
Interview with the man
who makes the
Emperor's new clothes

Time Out
The Drugs Explosion
An A-Z of Usage & Abusage

ABBEY ROAD
Look at Paul's feet

Abbey Road has an unchallenged place in the pantheon of album covers from the golden age of vinyl. It may lack the conceptual brilliance of Richard Hamilton's *White Album*, which transformed a plain envelope into a work of art by giving every copy a unique number. It doesn't have the energy of Peter Blake's *Sgt. Pepper* collage. But it did turn a previously mundane north London zebra crossing into a pilgrimage site for popular music's devout, one that is now protected by its English Heritage listing. Every available wall in the neighbourhood is covered in graffiti left by fans. The street signs are constantly being stolen.

The album image has been parodied and recreated countless times. Its occult meanings have been endlessly interrogated. Why is Paul barefoot? Why is Ringo wearing undertaker black? What is the significance of the 281F number plate on the Volkswagen Beetle parked in the background?

Abbey Road (1969) was the last album that the Beatles recorded together. The album cover was designed by John Kosh, the creative director of Apple Records, but the image of the four Beatles on the crossing outside the EMI recording studio was based on a sketch supposedly conceived by Paul McCartney himself. Iain Macmillan took the photograph on a hot August day in 1969 from the top of a stepladder positioned in the middle of the street, while a policeman held up the traffic. The back-cover image is another Macmillan photograph showing an Abbey Road street sign, although not one that comes from this stretch of the road.

The crossing that Macmillan photographed is in the borough of Westminster where street signs use black sans-serif type on white enamel with the borough name and the W9 postcode picked out in red. The Abbey Road sign on the back cover is from Hampstead. It is made, like many others in NW8, from individual serif letters, white on glossy black ceramic clay tiles, each of them carefully set into brick walls.

The cover of *Abbey Road* has inspired a huge number of alternative readings. Fans seek occult interpretations.

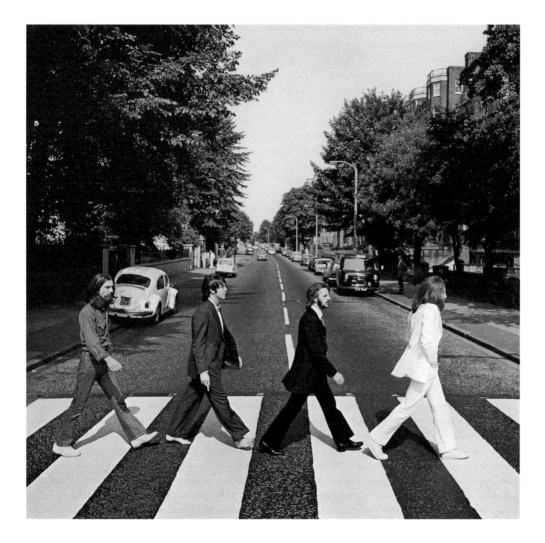

ARCHITECTURAL ASSOCIATION
Educating the architects

The world's only school exclusively devoted to architectural education is based in Bedford Square, a garden surrounded on four sides by dignified 18th-century houses that betray little sign of the generations of iconoclastic talent that have been nurtured inside number 36.

This was the school that nurtured Zaha Hadid and Richard Rogers, David Chipperfield and Ron Arad. It is the school that had Rem Koolhaas and Léon Krier on its teaching staff. Its graduates come from China and the United States, Malaysia and Australia, Greece and Germany.

While British architecture was at its lowest ebb in the 1970s and 1980s, the Architectural Association functioned as a kind of licensed opposition, a place that encouraged the exploration of new thinking. It is the place that trained the generation of architects who are now rebuilding London and exporting their work around the world.

Bedford Square is home to the Architectural Association, the world's largest school devoted entirely to architecture. Its graduates include Rem Koolhaas and Zaha Hadid.

LONDON IN FILM
Putting the city on screen

There is something a little pernicious about the way in which ambitious cities establish film offices and the accompanying slush funds to encourage producers to set up in their streets. It is always presented as a hardnosed business proposition that will attract investment and create jobs for an urban economy. But in fact it is really a much more narcissistic affair. It is like paying people to take your picture and put it in the paper.

London, by contrast, did not need to bribe Michelangelo Antonioni to come to London to film *Blowup* (1966) – he came of his own accord. He captured David Hemmings in his open-top Bentley with his car phone. He filmed him shooting Vanessa Redgrave in the Holland Park studio that later became Richard Rogers' architectural office. Nor did he need inducements to film Maria Schneider cast as an architecture student in *The Passenger* (1975) haunting the Brunswick Centre, Patrick Hodgkinson's extraordinary architectural insertion into Bloomsbury.

Hitchcock recreated Portland Place for *The 39 Steps* (1935) and Maida Vale for *Dial M for Murder* (1954). Stanley Kubrick came to London and set everything in his adopted city, from the bombed-out ruins of Hue that he recreated in the Docklands for *Full Metal Jacket* (1987), to the brutalist concrete of Thamesmead that he used as the backdrop for *A Clockwork Orange* (1971).

More recently, Anthony Minghella used King's Cross halfway through reconstruction as the setting for *Breaking and Entering* (2006), an exploration of the multiple layers of urban life in this rapidly gentrifying district, inhabited by Jude Law's landscape architect by day and at night by Kosovan drug dealers and Nigerian cleaners.

Stanley Kubrick explored many aspects of London in his films, none of them with more sinister impact than his use of the 1960s modernism of Thamesmead new town as the setting for *A Clockwork Orange* (1971).

BATTERSEA POWER STATION
A landmark redefined

Sir Giles Gilbert Scott belonged to an architectural dynasty that has made an indelible mark on London. His grandfather was responsible for the flamboyant red-brick St Pancras Station, and also the Albert Memorial, a gothic rocket built in tribute to Prince Albert by a grieving Queen Victoria. His father and his uncle both had distinguished architectural careers.

Giles Gilbert Scott was himself responsible for the cast-iron telephone boxes that were derived from the tomb of another famous architect, Sir John Soane (responsible for the Bank of England), and most conspicuously for two power stations on the Thames that kept London in electricity for much of the 20th century. One, at Bankside, is now Tate Modern. The other, at Battersea, has been made famous far beyond London by the starring role it played on Pink Floyd's *Animals* (1977) album cover, involving, in the days before digitally manipulated artwork, a giant inflatable pig that was floated above the structure.

Once regarded as an eyesore, and compared to a giant upturned table, the structure is now a listed landmark, though finding a new use has seen the bankruptcy of a series of developers over the last three decades. A project that involves building housing by Norman Foster, Frank Gehry and others is now inching towards being realized.

Battersea Power Station's four chimneys were once considered an eyesore. Pink Floyd's *Animals* album cover helped make them a landmark that is now protected.

M25
London Orbital

Britain came late to motorways. It was only in 1959, long after Germany's autobahns and the United States' parkway-building programmes had taken shape that Britain finally started developing its own version. The M25 orbital, London's distinctive contribution to motorway building, came even later. It may owe something to Washington, DC's Beltway, or the Boulevard Périphérique in Paris, but it is the largest of its kind in Europe and serves to define the shape and the identity of the city.

For better or worse, the M25 has come to be seen as London's defining limit, somewhere between a city wall and a high street.

The M25 is the product of an endlessly drawn-out planning process. The original idea was to restructure London around a set of four concentric motorway boxes that would have seen the wholesale destruction of swathes of historic buildings in Covent Garden and family homes in the inner suburbs. After a massive protest campaign the bulldozers were called off, and only the least destructive, outermost ring was completed.

It took 15 years to finish the 118km (73 miles) of the M25 that now serve to define London. It does not reflect political or geographical boundaries but, by default, sums up London as a post-industrial city, an amorphous sprawl that spans ancient settlements and open space, business parks and out-of-town shopping malls, binding them together into a more or less coherent single entity.

The M25 has had the effect of generating, rather than taming, traffic. From its original six lanes, it has fattened into eight and then ten. There was even a plan to widen the section near Heathrow to 14 lanes. Jock Kinneir and Margaret Calvert devised the signage system in time for the first motorways in 1959, and this still provides the organizing thread for Britain's roads. In the M25 signs, they have given London an instantly recognizable welcome mat.

London Orbital
M25
The North
Rick'worth 6
Amersham 12
Watford 12
Harlow 44

LLOYD'S OF LONDON
High tech's cathedral

The Pompidou Centre in Paris, built with his then partner, Renzo Piano, made Richard Rogers one of the world's most famous architects. But after it was completed, work dried up. Rogers was on the verge of leaving Britain to take up a teaching role in the United States when he won the competition to design the third headquarters for the Lloyd's of London insurance market to be built in less than a century.

Rogers' design was a startling intrusion in the Square Mile when it was completed. But this was, despite its appearance, in fact a surprisingly traditional project. It was not, like so many of the new office buildings in London, a speculative project designed with no specific occupant in mind. It was entirely designed for the purposes of its owner and user. It was a Savile Row tailor-made suit, albeit one of a somewhat eccentric cut.

Lloyd's looked startlingly new but it was built before the digital revolution changed the nature of financial transactions. It was built before the scandals that left the reputation of Lloyd's in tatters, as the 'names' – private individuals who made their capital available for insurance underwriting – found that they were allocated to high-risk syndicates and lost everything.

The building is a listed monument now, accorded the same protection as a neoclassical royal palace or a gothic cathedral. Just as well, given the degree to which the technology on which it depends has changed.

Lloyd's of London is the insurance market that began as a coffee house and became a financial institution. Richard Rogers gave it a new home in the 1980s so distinctive that it is now a listed landmark.

FULCRUM BY RICHARD SERRA
A new monument

The Broadgate development took what had once been two Victorian railway stations, Liverpool Street and Broad Street, and transformed them into 370,000 square metres (four million square feet) of prime office space. It was a project that played an important part in making life difficult for the developers of Canary Wharf. It was also notable for the quality of its architecture – initiated by the late Peter Foggo of Arup Associates, then taken forward by the US firm Skidmore, Owings & Merrill (SOM) – and its public spaces featuring travertine and bronze and even a skating rink. By an impressive sleight of hand, the authorities were persuaded to allow a change in the postcode boundaries – giving the offices a vital EC postal code that signified prime financial territory, rather than fringe.

Broadgate is also the scene of one of London's very few pieces of wholly convincing public art – Richard Serra's *Fulcrum*, five sheets of COR-TEN steel, 17m (56ft) high.

When the City of London's financial core was expanded northward by building on top of the tracks at Liverpool Street Station, Richard Serra was commissioned to make an artwork that reflected the civic ambition of the project.

BLUE PLAQUES
Making his own mark

There are now nearly 900 plaques affixed to buildings in London recording their association with notable individuals. They date back to 1867 and a scheme put forward by the Royal Society of Arts and enthusiastically endorsed by Henry Cole, father of the Crystal Palace and the Victoria and Albert Museum. The oldest surviving sign marks the house in Covent Garden in which an exiled Napoleon III lived until he returned to Paris. Others commemorate an extraordinary range of individuals, from Karl Marx in Soho and Friedrich Engels in Primrose Hill, to Vivien Leigh, Mozart and Handel. There is a suburban semi-detached house with a memorial to the first British soldier to enter the gates of the liberated Auschwitz. And a plaque on the side of New Zealand House commemorates the communist revolutionary Prime Minister Ho Chi Minh, who before returning to Vietnam worked as a waiter in a restaurant that once stood on the site.

They are generally called 'blue plaques', though in the early days they could be terracotta coloured. They have been successfully administered by the London County Council, the Greater London Council and English Heritage. For many years the ceramic was manufactured by Royal Doulton; more recently, they have been made by individual craftspeople. In 1991 the Royal College of Art refused Gavin Turk a degree on the basis that his final show, 'Cave', consisted of a whitewashed studio space containing only a blue heritage plaque commemorating his own presence: 'GAVIN TURK Sculptor worked here 1989–1991'.

Ceramic plaques, sometimes blue and sometimes terracotta, have been used to define the historic associations of London addresses for more than a century. Gavin Turk made his own when he was an art student (below).

CANARY WHARF
Why is it so high?

London has been shaped as much by a series of unintended consequences as by positive planning. Canary Wharf was once at the heart of one of the busiest ports in the world. The invention of the shipping container had the impact of a neutron bomb, not just on London but also on every upstream dock in the world. Within two decades the hundreds of dockland acres, once crammed with shipping and tens of thousands of dockers, were empty; the basins mirror-smooth, disturbed only by the occasional seagull.

London's politicians seemed unable to deal with the scale of the transformation. At one point, the Greater London Council seriously debated turning the whole area into a giant park, so doubtful was it about its ability to attract new industries, or even new residents, into the locale. Finally, Michael Heseltine, Mrs Thatcher's environment minister, designated the area an enterprise zone, with tax incentives and streamlined planning controls, in a bid to attract the light-industrial sheds that he believed was all it could hope for.

Then, in one of those great historical accidents, a banker from Credit Suisse First Boston was taken to the area by a restaurateur looking for the funding to build a warehouse to serve his business. The banker realized that exactly the same incentives would apply to a skyscraper as to a crinkly tin shed. And so the new business district of Canary Wharf was born.

'Why does it have to be so tall?', asked the Prince of Wales of One Canada Square, the first major tower in the Docklands and the work of American architect César Pelli. The answer Pelli was too polite to give was simple: it was a signpost to tell the world where Canary Wharf was. It is hardly lovely, but Pelli's key decision – to persuade his clients, the Reichmann brothers, not to clad the building in the stone that they asked for but to use aluminium – was a move that gave the tower a life and character. Against a dark sky it looks light; against sunshine it is dark. When completed it was a solitary monolith, a singular quality that it has now lost as a thicket of subsequent towers has surrounded it.

London's biggest transformation in a century was the move eastward of its finance sector with the construction of the Canary Wharf office development. César Pelli's tower was built tall enough to signal its presence.

NO. 1 POULTRY
Modern cities

Not a fashionable name today, but James Stirling during his lifetime was regarded as the most significant British architect since Edwin Lutyens. No. 1 Poultry, somewhat mysteriously and with no intention of flattery, was described by the Prince of Wales as looking like a 1930s wireless. Somewhat ungenerous of him, given that it was only built when the planners changed their minds and turned against the glass tower that Mies van der Rohe had designed for the same site.

The future of this one site was a lightning rod for all the planning debates of the late 20th century, when 19th-century buildings went from dispensable to heritage, and arguments about how to replace them fluctuated from fitting in with the context to a wholesale remodelling.

Stirling began his career in the 1960s with a series of brick-and-glass university buildings – notably in Leicester, Cambridge and Oxford – that were a mixture of industrial vernacular and Russian constructivism. By the time of the No. 1 Poultry project Stirling had begun to explore a more historicist approach to architecture, bringing together elements from various periods to create a kind of collage, planned around a dramatic open-topped drum.

The Stirling scheme features the Coq d'Argent restaurant, with a rooftop garden that offers some of the most striking views of the City, and in particular of the Lutyens-designed former Midland Bank head office just across the street.

James Stirling, with partner Michael Wilford, was the architect of No. 1 Poultry, a site that for years was the focus for a battle between alternative views of how London should grow. The Prince of Wales torpedoed a previous project designed by Mies van der Rohe, but failed to stop Stirling.

PAUL SMITH AT WESTBOURNE HOUSE
A home for fashion

At the end of the 1970s when Covent Garden was in its last days as a fruit and vegetable market, long before it had turned into a focus for tourists, Paul Smith already had it in his sights as the place for his first shop in London. It was in Floral Street, and he opened when all around was still dereliction.

Then Smith expanded into a far more playful incarnation in fashionable Notting Hill. He took over a white stucco Victorian house – used as a restaurant until Smith acquired it – and, working with the architect Sophie Hicks, turned it into a new model for what a shop might be, one that has been remarkably influential throughout the world.

On the ground floor there are children's toys and carefully selected second-hand books and vintage magazines. On the top floor is a made-to-measure bespoke suit-making business. The stairs between are crammed with photographs, posters and art from Smith's personal collection.

Paul Smith's largest shop in London transformed a white stucco-fronted building off the Portobello Road, but maintained its domestic character.

SERPENTINE PAVILION
Pavilion architects

The Serpentine Gallery occupies what was once a ladylike neoclassical tearoom in Kensington Gardens, not far from the original site of Joseph Paxton's Crystal Palace. Since it was transformed from its original purpose into a gallery, it has played an essential role in making contemporary art socially acceptable in London. It is a place where smart Londoners and moneyed art collectors come to explore some of the wilder shores of art. The patronage of the late Princess of Wales made it a paparazzi magnet. She was photographed looking glamorous on her way to a party here on the night that a shamefaced Prince of Wales went on national television to talk about his shortcomings as a husband.

Since 1999 the Serpentine has worked hard to make contemporary architecture part of the wider cultural agenda too. Each year the director, Julia Peyton-Jones, invites an architect who has not previously built in Britain to design a temporary pavilion for the gallery. The brief is loose, but the pavilion must be capable of being used as a café and a meeting space for the summer. It is then dismantled and sold on to help pay for the cost of the project.

Over the years there have been pavilions by such veterans as Oscar Niemeyer and Frank Gehry, as well as by younger talents. It has given Londoners the chance to see work by Toyo Ito and Álvaro Siza Vieira at first hand. Peter Zumthor created a carefully planted garden of weeds, caught in a mute black perimeter wall. Over the years the no-previous-British-projects rule has been relaxed. Jacques Herzog and Pierre de Meuron worked with Ai Weiwei after they completed Tate Modern, creating a cork-lined archaeological excavation. Rem Koolhaas built an inflatable plastic bubble that turned out to be one of the more difficult pavilions to sell on.

The Serpentine Gallery added architecture to its repertoire of contemporary art by commissioning architects including (clockwise from top left) Peter Zumthor, Frank Gehry, Oscar Niemeyer and Sou Fujimoto to design temporary pavilions.

76

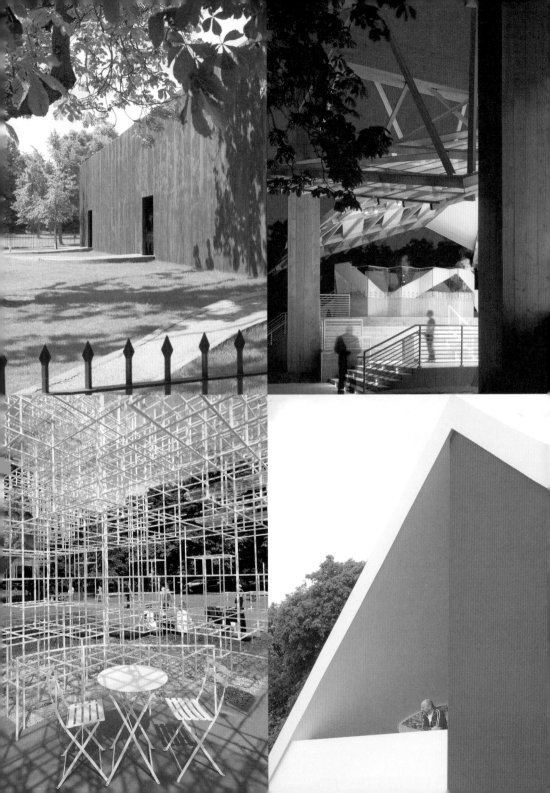

LORD'S
The home of cricket

Lord's Cricket Ground, which celebrated its 200th anniversary in 2014 and is owned by the Marylebone Cricket Club, has turned out to be one of London's more unexpected patrons of contemporary architecture. In the midst of the trappings of the international home of cricket, Lord's has acquired a sequence of new stands and amenities, designed by Michael Hopkins and Nicholas Grimshaw, and culminating in the Media Centre, the work of Future Systems – the late Jan Kaplicky and his partner, Amanda Levete.

The dominant language is a polite high-tech, but the Media Centre, which won Future Systems the Stirling Prize, is the most striking and original. It uses a semi-monocoque structure that uses the skin for strength and stability and does away with the need for internal columns. It was built in Cornwall by a boatyard and shipped to London for assembly. Hoisted on stilts, it looks as though it is floating above one of the stands, a sleek flying saucer sliced through by a window wall to give commentators an unobstructed view of the pitch. The skin is punctuated at the back and on top by a pattern of circular openings. The interior is full of saturated colour and curved surfaces.

Lord's Cricket Ground has distinguished itself by commissioning a range of contemporary architects to remodel its stands, and in particular by giving Future Systems the job of building its media centre.

TATE TURBINE HALL
When art draws the crowds

The huge brick cliff designed by Giles Gilbert Scott to house central London's last electricity-generating power station had a surprisingly short life. It started generating power in 1952 and had been superseded by 1981 when it closed. It occupied an extraordinary riverside site, however, directly opposite St Paul's Cathedral. Its chimney, at 99m (325ft), was carefully designed so as not to be as tall as Christopher Wren's dome.

Its transformation into the world's most visited gallery of contemporary art was the product of Tate director Sir Nicholas Serota's inspired decision that the restricted nature of Tate's original site at Millbank meant that it had to find somewhere else to expand. And, by moving to another site, logic determined a reorganization of its collections. Millbank became Tate Britain, with holdings from Holbein to Caulfield by way of Turner. Bankside became Tate Modern, causing Britain's living artists to agonize over where they would rather be shown.

Serota ran a competition to find an architect and chose the Basel-based practice Herzog & de Meuron. For them it would prove the first high-profile international step on a trajectory that would end up with their design of the stadium for the Beijing Olympic Games.

The new gallery succeeded beyond all expectations, with 4 million visitors in its first year (25 per cent above predictions) – attracted by the Turbine Hall and its spectacular installations by Louise Bourgeois, Olafur Eliasson and others, and by the new pedestrian bridge across the Thames, designed by Norman Foster, which quickly recovered from its initial tendency to wobble under the feet of the pedestrians who flocked to use it. In the process, the centuries-long psychological barrier that divided north London from south was erased. Southwark – for so long the Ciudad Juárez on the south bank to the El Paso of the north – had become respectable.

The move of the Tate modern collection to the former Bankside power station has revitalized London's south bank, and hugely increased public interest in contemporary art.

MILLENNIUM BRIDGE
The bridge that wobbled

This is the bridge that famously wobbled. Devised by architect Norman Foster and the engineers of Arup, with some sculptural input from artist Anthony Caro, the Millennium Bridge, as it is officially known, was built to connect Tate Modern with the north bank of the Thames. Crossing it provides a remarkable view: north towards the dome of St Paul's, with which it is aligned, and both east and west along the river. The design was selected as the result of a competition. Foster's team focused on creating a bridge that made as little of a mark on the skyline as possible.

It was closed within 24 hours of opening when the large crowds attempting to cross provoked an unexpected movement in what, despite its low profile, is a suspension bridge supported by cables. The bridge started to sway perceptibly, an effect that increased as pedestrians responded by bracing themselves against it.

The engineers went back to the calculations and found that, while the bridge was structurally safe, the larger the crowds the more pronounced the wobble became. It was retrofitted with additional stabilizers and shock absorbers to minimize the impact of thousands of footsteps moving in unison, and reopened after a year with the judder removed and the structure rendered stable.

When the Millennium Bridge opened in 2000, it wobbled embarrassingly and was temporarily closed. The structural problem has been solved, and the bridge is today a key link between north and south banks.

THE HOUSE OF THE ARTIST
A new artists' quarter

When Damien Hirst, Tracey Emin and a handful of other former 'Young British Artists', many of whom had studied with Michael Craig-Martin at Goldsmiths, first attracted the attention of the fledgling art collector Charles Saatchi, for the most part London's artists were dependent on teaching or the dole for survival. At the end of the 1980s the outermost edge of fashionable London stopped well short of any postcode that started with an E.

The explosion of the art market, fuelled by a wave of new City money, transformed both the social geography of London and the status of its artists. A handful of them were suddenly affluent enough to be able to build their own studio houses.

The last time that London had seen anything like it was when the Pre-Raphaelites had been accepted into the Royal Academy, and made enough from selling their paintings to be able to commission the fashionable architects of the day to build them prodigious studio houses in Holland Park. George Aitchison built Lord Leighton a particularly spectacular example in the form of a Moorish palace.

A century later some artists were making enough to hire David Adjaye. But these studios were on the other side of London from their Pre-Raphaelite predecessors. The Dirty House that David Adjaye designed for post-YBA duo Tim Noble and Sue Webster, on the edge of Hoxton, was surrounded by some of the less desirable traces of East End real life when it was completed, which made the protective anti-climb paint a necessary precaution.

In the 19th century London's most successful artists built houses in Chelsea. Now they live in the east of the city and some use David Adjaye to design their homes.

CITY HALL
A new home for a new mayor

The visible seat of civic authority in London was once County Hall, an eruption of Edwardian baroque splendour south of the Thames, just across Westminster Bridge from the Houses of Parliament. County Hall was built as the home of the London County Council and its architectural challenge to Westminster was a clear assertion of its ambition to be taken seriously. The council's successor, the Greater London Council, was abolished by the Conservative government of Margaret Thatcher, and its former home sold off at a discount to new owners, who have since turned it into a hotel and a series of tourist attractions, including an aquarium.

City Hall, London's most recent seat of power, re-emerged with the establishment of the Greater London Authority by Prime Minister Tony Blair in the 1990s. Its home was designed by Norman Foster's office and sits on the south bank. It was the product of a commercial development – a civic structure built in the midst of an office campus.

Its sculptural form marked a shift in Foster's architectural approach. Its interior is a continuous spiral wrapped around the debating chamber, with offices above and meeting rooms beneath. The building might be understood as reflecting a form of local government that has been based as much on the personality of the mayor as on party issues.

When London acquired a mayor in the early years of the 21st century, Norman Foster's City Hall helped to define the identity of the new institution.

THE WOLSELEY
Tables of power

Restaurants designed by architects have not, by and large, enjoyed much longevity in London. David Chipperfield's reworking of the Café Royal mixed a carefully exact restoration of the historic rooms with a refined yet bracingly austere restaurant that was quickly softened by its owner. John Pawson's sushi bar in West Hampstead was blown up by an IRA bomb. Carmody Groarke – a practice founded by former employees of Chipperfield – caught the Zeitgeist for the pop-up when they elegantly transformed a filling station in the midst of the King's Cross redevelopment into a temporary restaurant. Perhaps the most successful combination of architecture and eating was Eva Jiricna's recreation of Le Caprice.

More typical is the Wolseley, the work of the late David Collins, in which a former car showroom has been turned into a smart London's dining room. With a vaulted scale that somehow suggests the set for one of Errol Flynn's more swashbuckling films, the Wolseley is planned around an inner circle – where Lucien Freud's regular table was marked by a candle on the day that he died – and an outer ring of tables that define social Siberia.

Restaurants have become the civic landmarks of London. They are the places to meet others, to parade in public. The Wolseley, once a car showroom, is the most conspicuous example of the type. Breakfast here is a ritual for the media and financial elite.

HAYWARD GALLERY UNDERCROFT
Skateboard city

For most of the 1980s and the 1990s the South Bank Arts Centre was inevitably described as a windswept barren concrete wasteland. If that was ever true, it certainly isn't now, with the riverside walkway overwhelmed by people, outdoor food stalls, and a wave of shopping outlets lapping at the edges of the concert halls and theatres that line the Thames from the former County Hall to the National Theatre.

The transformation of what was once an industrial area began in the aftermath of World War II. In 1951 the Festival of Britain occupied most of the site, with bomb-damaged ruins and redundant warehouses swept aside to make way for temporary structures. The one permanent building, the Royal Festival Hall, still stands, conceived as a village hall for the capital, with multiple auditoriums, a poetry library, meeting rooms and cafés. Then came the Queen Elizabeth Hall, with its two concert halls, and the Hayward Gallery, completed in 1968, and finally the National Theatre, opened in 1976.

Both the Festival Hall and the Hayward complex were designed by the London County Council Architects' Department. The Festival Hall is a polite, slightly Scandinavian-inflected piece of contemporary modernism. The Hayward is a much more striking, confrontational work, designed by a team that included Warren Chalk, Ron Herron and Dennis Crompton. Outside working hours, they joined Peter Cook to set up Archigram, one of Britain's more playful, futurist-inclined architectural studios.

Every decade or so there have been misguided attempts to demolish or rework the South Bank, even as its architectural qualities are once more being appreciated. But the most recent attempt at an unsympathetic makeover was defeated not by an appreciation of the architecture of the 1960s, but by a concerted campaign by skateboarders to maintain their presence on the ramps and slopes of the undercroft.

When the South Bank Centre was being completed in the 1960s, its site was always presented as an empty wasteland. It has since become one of London's most popular public spaces.

'ONE CITY UNDER CCTV'
Surveillance city

Banksy is not a Londoner; his roots are in Bristol. And he is far from being the only artist to have made CCTV cameras the subject of his work. Ai Weiwei monumentalized his experience of being kept under continuous observation by the Chinese government much more poignantly – with a marble version of a surveillance camera in 2010 – and has paid a personal price in a way that Banksy has never had to.

The graffiti artist who makes a fetish of keeping his identity secret and trades on an outlaw image, even now that his work sells for six-figure sums at respectable auction houses, frequently returns to the theme in his works in London. There was a particularly conspicuous example on the wall of a Post Office sorting yard close to Oxford Street that involved him climbing temporary scaffolding to paint the words 'One Nation Under CCTV' in letters 1m (3ft) high. While it was quickly obliterated, there are still a number of his signature stencil-style works featuring surveillance cameras throughout the capital.

Given that London has one of the highest concentrations of surveillance cameras in the world, it is a particularly appropriate motif. London's 33 local authorities say that they operate 7,000 CCTV cameras between them, which compares with fewer than 600 in Paris. Other figures suggest that there is one camera for every 11 Londoners.

One of London's most defining uses of cameras is in its congestion charging system. After Singapore, it has the world's most extensive and most sophisticated system for making motorists pay to drive into the city centre. This depends on cameras positioned at every access point, each of which has the ability to read and recognize individual licence plates. The initial unintended consequence was a spate of number plate thefts.

Banksy has left his distinctive mark all across London, here referring to the city's fascination with surveillance cameras.

WHITE CUBE, BERMONDSEY
Art central

Apart from vertiginous housing costs, and a conspicuous improvement in the quality and ambition of its restaurants, the emphasis on contemporary art is one of the most notable aspects of London's transformation in the last two decades into a global centre for footloose capital.

Until the 1990s contemporary art was a kind of cult in London, confined to the art schools: a dissident, poverty-struck minority interest. The arrival of an art market saw the creation of a number of institutions to cater to it. There is the Frieze Art Fair, established by Matthew Slotover in a tent in the Regent's Park, and a clutch of new dealers with deep enough pockets to create premises that eclipse anything that a public museum can offer. Larry Gagosian opened a sequence of spaces in King's Cross and in Mayfair. And Jay Jopling, the Old Etonian director of the White Cube, began life in Masons' Yard in the West End and in Hoxton Square.

Jopling's move from Hoxton to Bermondsey prompted a wave of speculation about the capital's art world moving south of the river. In its Bermondsey incarnation, the White Cube shows its artists, from Antony Gormley to Marc Quinn, in a series of spectacular spaces.

Art dealer Jay Jopling's White Cube gallery on Bermondsey High Street has helped transform this once neglected part of south London. Its size and scale reflects the increasing financial clout of the contemporary art market. White Cube's architects were Casper Mueller Kneer.

LONDON AQUATICS CENTRE
Olympic legacies

One of the more endearing aspects of Londoners is their reluctance to embrace the obvious. Thus, when the International Olympics Committee named London as the seat of the 2012 Games, the immediate reaction of a sizable number of Londoners was not celebration, but a heartfelt wish that Paris had won instead. In the event, the city decided that, on the whole, it thoroughly enjoyed the experience despite such troubling issues as an Olympics-only traffic lane.

One of the key projects that secured the Games for London was the commitment to build an aquatics centre designed by Zaha Hadid. The pool is topped by a spectacular roof that seems to float weightlessly above it, sheltering a sculptural diving board. During the Games the pool sprouted ungainly wings to accommodate the required 80,000 spectators. In its slimmed-down form it is now a much appreciated neighbourhood swimming pool, a landmark in the transformation of Stratford in particular, and east London in general. For generations, this area – like the eastern approaches of so many cities – was socially disadvantaged. For London, this is no longer true. The investment in the Olympic Park, with its village and new transport links, has capitalized on a new turn to the east for the city.

The 2012 Olympics triggered the development of Stratford. The Olympic village is now used for rental housing, the stadium for football and Zaha Hadid's striking pool is used by the community.

MOUNT STREET
Conspicuous consumption

Every decade or so, London grows a new street that becomes a front line for fashionable society. In the 1960s the King's Road eclipsed Carnaby Street. In the 1980s Bond Street vied with Sloane Street.

Mount Street, once a staid Mayfair enclave far beyond the reach of fashion, is now the centre of a feeding frenzy – with the revitalized Connaught Hotel and its Tadao Ando fountain at one end and Scott's at the other. Scott's, the restaurant outside which Charles Saatchi was photographed seemingly holding Nigella Lawson, then his wife, by the neck, has turned into the official parade ground of the leisured classes. Here they gather, bent on their careers of conspicuous consumption, in much the same way that their 19th-century predecessors might once have navigated Hyde Park in their open carriages.

In between the Connaught and Scott's are a selection of the most over-heatedly fashionable London stores, all the way from John Pawson's shop for Christopher Kane at one end to Christian Louboutin and Marc by Marc Jacobs, by way of Roksanda Ilincic, at the other.

With Tadao Ando's pool outside the Connaught Hotel at one end, and Scott's restaurant at the other, Mount Street has become a parade ground for conspicuous consumers.

CENTRAL LONDON'S SKYSCRAPERS
The march of the high rises

Almost unnoticed now in the eruption of towers that has spread across central and east London are the stainless-steel mullions of what was once called the NatWest Tower, after the bank whose headquarters used to occupy the building and on whose logotype the floor plan was based. It is called Tower 42 now – a reference to the street address, but hinting also at how much London's relationship with tall buildings has changed. For a decade Richard Seifert's provincial attempt at a skyscraper was the tallest building in Britain, visible from 10km (6 miles) away, dominating views of the city.

Then, at the turn of the century, the presumption that London was a predominantly low-rise city was abandoned, and a sequence of ever more attention-seeking, and often – as in the case of the residential tower on top of Nine Elms (the new location for the US Embassy) – crude, high rises climbed above the city.

Norman Foster's tower for Swiss Re, officially 30 St Mary Axe, in memory of the medieval street on which it was built, but inevitably described as the 'Gherkin', reset the game. The era of the Miesian-influenced glass box was at an end.

For a while the Gherkin stood in isolation. That moment has gone now, and for the time being it is the towers built by two former partners, Renzo Piano and Richard Rogers, that dominate central London – Piano's eroded pyramidal form (The Shard) on the south bank at London Bridge, and Rogers' 'Cheese grater' (122 Leadenhall St) on the north bank, directly opposite the firm's now-listed Lloyd's Building. Between the two is the misshapen lump that is Rafael Viñoly's so-called 'Walkie-Talkie' (20 Fenchurch St), a swelling confection without merit whose worst offence is that, when looking up river from the east, it completely fills the frame formed by Tower Bridge.

The crop of skyscrapers that has transformed London's skyline would have been inconceivable before the building of Canary Wharf. Planning policies that banned them were overturned in an attempt to compete. Richard Rogers' so-called 'Cheese grater' is the most impressive new arrival.

59 BRICK LANE
From chapel to mosque

What is now a mosque at 59 Brick Lane was once a synagogue and, before that, a Methodist chapel, but was originally built as a Huguenot place of worship in 1743. If one single building can represent the essence of London's cultural diversity of three centuries, this is it.

Brick Lane, now the centre of the city's Bangladeshi community, was once an area of weavers' lofts – domestic family factories run by French Huguenots, Protestant refugees from France's murderous Wars of Religion. Their presence lingers only in a few additions to the area's 18th-century houses, built to accommodate their looms, and in the form of this brick building on the corner of Brick Lane and Fournier Street. It has a minaret now and is operated as a mosque, but it was built by the French in a plain but handsome brick style. And in between its life as a chapel and as a mosque it was, for more than a century, a synagogue – established by Eastern European Jews fleeing Russian pogroms.

The transformation of this one building is mirrored by that of the city around it. Street signs are now rendered in Bengali, even as the 18th-century weavers' houses have been restored by wealthy newcomers, as the city's financial centre presses ever eastward into Spitalfields.

Vibrant Brick Lane, just to the east of the City of London's financial centre, has housed successive migrant communities since the 17th century.

A NEW DESIGN MUSEUM
An icon reborn

In the wake of the completion of Frank Gehry's outpost for the Guggenheim in Bilbao, there was a rush of new museums attempting to construct themselves equally conspicuous, attention-hogging iconic buildings, a process that had diminishing returns.

When the Design Museum outgrew its first home, a converted banana-ripening warehouse next to Tower Bridge, it acquired the former Commonwealth Institute, a building striking enough for the museum not to need to strive self-consciously to build a new icon. All it had to do was bring an existing one back to life.

The original institute was opened by Queen Elizabeth II in 1962. It was designed by Robert Matthew Johnson-Marshall, while the interiors were the work of James Gardner, who had also worked on the Festival of Britain. It was one of the first pieces of contemporary architecture completed in London after post-war rationing ended, replacing the Imperial Institute, a handsome Victorian structure on Exhibition Road, South Kensington. Behind its blue-glass skin and its copper roof, it looked strikingly contemporary.

John Pawson's remodelling of the interior maintains the essential spatial qualities of the original building, with its spectacular roof – a hyperbolic paraboloid concrete shell. And it is still organized around a central void. At the same time it allows for the new use of the building, a place in which the museum's permanent collection will be on show, alongside galleries showing temporary exhibitions. Pawson's interior maintains the original materials as much as possible, but gently revitalizes it with oak and terrazzo finishes.

The former Commonwealth Institute, completed in 1962, is now the home of the Design Museum, remodelled by John Pawson.

THE SKYLINE
City on a river

Anonymous cities have generic skylines in which the only distinguishing marks are the brand names on top of hotels, on street signs and in neon advertising signs. Distinctive cities define themselves by the recognizable patterns that their buildings make, the way that they look at different times of day, silhouetted against the sun or cloud, their relationship with the landscape.

London's skyline is still anchored by the handful of monuments that have shaped it for centuries. The Tower of London is the oldest, followed, at a distance of some centuries, by Westminster Abbey, then by St Paul's Cathedral. After that came the fretwork gothic of Sir Charles Barry and Augustus Pugin's Houses of Parliament, and the curious blend of Victorian engineering and baronial imagery that is Tower Bridge. The most recent landmark in this tradition is the London Eye, intended as a temporary celebration of the Millennium but now a permanent fixture that quickly made itself an essential London landmark.

But the skyline – despite the measure of continuity provided by the protected sightlines that are intended to keep the dome of St Paul's uncompromised by new development – is continually changing, now more than ever. Despite its reputation as a conservative, tradition-bound city, London is in the midst of a planning free-for-all that is seeing its skyline continually metamorphosing with the accelerated dispatch of a speeded-up time-lapse film. Clusters of towers are now erupting on top of the key transport interchanges, and with a speed and ruthlessness that makes London the closest thing that Europe has to Shanghai.

London is defined by its river. Water transforms the quality of light in the city that Charles Dickens wrote about and the twists of the river create its distinctive skyline. Spreading east of St Paul's, London now has a larger cluster of tall buildings than any other European city.

INDEX

PICTURE CREDITS

The publisher would like to thank the following contributors for their kind permission to reproduce the following photographs:

2 Bildarchiv Monheim GmbH/Alamy; 7 Pefkos/ Shutterstock; 9 Guildhall Library & Art Gallery/ Heritage Images/Getty Images; 10 Latitude Stock/ Alamy; 11 John Gay/English Heritage/NMR/Mary Evans Picture Library; 12 Ron Ellis/ Shutterstock; 13 Claudio Divizia/Shutterstock; 14 Sipsmith Independent Spirits; 15 Wellcome Library, London; 16 Richard Bryant/Arcaid/ Alamy; 17 Nigel Dickinson/ Alamy; 18 Heritage Images/ Hulton Archive/Getty Images; 19 LondonStills.com; 20 English Heritage/Arcaid/ Corbis; 21 Markus Lange/ Imagebroker/Alamy; 23 Peter Durant/Arcaid/Alamy; 25 Prisma Bildagentur AG/ Alamy; 26 Travel Pictures/ Alamy; 27 Mary Evans Picture Library/Alamy; 28 G Jackson/Arcaid/Alamy; 29 TfL from the London Transport Museum collection; 30 use of trademark courtesy Chelsea Football Club; 31 Don Morley/Getty Images; 33 J R James Archive/ University of Sheffield; 35 Popperfoto/Getty Images; 37 photo by Karl Adamson © Octopus Publishing Group, reproduced by permission of Penguin Books Ltd; 38 Ron Ellis/Shutterstock; 39 Bikeworldtravel/Shutterstock; 40 John Murray/Picture Post/ Getty Images; 41 Popperfoto/ Getty Images; 43 I R Stone / Shutterstock; 45 TopFoto; 47 Hufton + Crow/View Pictures/ Alamy; 49 View Pictures/ UIG via Getty Images; 51 Nick Ansell/PA Wire/ Press Association Images; 52, 53 courtesy Time Out; 55 © Apple Corps Ltd; 57 View Pictures/UIG via Getty Images; 59 Warner Brothers/ The Kobal Collection; 61 CBW/Alamy; 63 Photofusion/ Rex Features; 64 Pawel Toczynski/Getty Images; 65 Hugh Nutt/Alamy; 67 PSL Images/Alamy; 68 Cavey 1991-7 by Gavin Turk. Live Stock Market/Tate, London 2015; 69 Hulton Archive/ Getty Images; 71 D Burke/ Alamy; 72 Brian Harris/Rex Features; 73 Pawel Libera/ Corbis; 75 Paul Smith, Westbourne House; 76 Anthony Shaw Photography/ Shutterstock; 77 al, ar & br View Pictures/UIG via Getty Images; 77 bl Ron Ellis/ Shutterstock; 79 Arcaid/UIG via Getty Images; 80 Brian Harris/Rex Features; 81 The Weather Project, 2003, by Olafur Eliasson. Tate, London 2015; 83 Dennis Gilbert/Vew Pictures; 85 Daniel Hewitt/ View Pictures/Alamy; 86 Jose Fuste Raga/Corbis; 87 D Burke/Alamy; 89 Corbin & King; 91 Londonstills. com/SuperStock; 93 Chris Dorney/Shutterstock; 95 Paul Riddle/View Pictures/Alamy; 97 Hufton + Crow/View Pictures; 99 Jonathan Player/ Rex Features; 101 Vladimir Zakharov/Getty Images; 103 Eurasia Press/Getty Images; 104 Jimmy Sime/Hulton Archive/Getty Images; 105 Alex Morris Visualisation; 107 Jack Taylor/Rex Features.

CREDITS

An Hachette UK Company
www.hachette.co.uk

First published in
Great Britain in 2015
by Conran Octopus,
a division of Octopus
Publishing Group Ltd
in conjunction with the
Design Museum

Octopus Publishing Group Ltd
Carmelite House
50 Victoria Embankment
London EC4Y 0DZ
www.octopusbooks.co.uk
www.octopusbooksusa.com

Copyright © Octopus
Publishing Group Ltd 2015

Distributed in the US by
Hachette Book Group
1290 Avenue of the
Americas, 4th and 5th Floors,
New York, NY 10020

Distributed in Canada by
Canadian Manda Group
664 Annette St., Toronto,
Ontario, Canada M6S 2C8

A CIP catalogue record
for this book is available
from the British Library.

Text written by:
Deyan Sudjic

Commissioning Editor:
Joe Cottington
Editor:
Pollyanna Poulter
Copy Editor:
Robert Anderson
Design:
Untitled
Picture Researcher:
Claire Hamilton
Production Controller:
Sarah Kramer

Based on a concept by
Hugh Devlin

Printed and bound in China
ISBN 978 1 84091 692 8

10 9 8 7 6 5 4 3 2 1